KAKA'S AFRICAN FABLE
EXCITING SHORT STORIES

KAKA'S AFRICAN FABLE
EXCITING SHORT STORIES

KAKA ANTHONY

DEDICATION

This book is dedicated to people all over the world who enjoys fable and fictional stories.

INTRODUCTION

Oral stories had been passed down from generation to generation. Some of these stories have been lost over the years because they were not documented. Kaka Anthony uses *Kaka's African Fable* to put into writing and to bring back to life some of these fables to be enjoyed by adults and children.

TABLE OF CONTENT

CHAPTER ONE

Tortoise and the Magic Plate - 6

CHAPTER TWO

Mr. Okoro and the Rats - 18

CHAPTER THREE

Why is Fowl used for Sacrifice? - 26

TABLE OF CONTENTS

CHAPTER ONE

Itenchia and the Major Male 6

CHAPTER TWO

Mr. Okoro and the Rats 14

CHAPTER THREE

Wrong Love Wrong Sacrifice 26

CHAPTER ONE

TORTOISE AND THE MAGIC PLATE

Once upon a time, in the animal kingdom, rain had refused to fall for a long time and because of this, the crops began to die; all the green grasses and leaves were dried up. There was no food anywhere for the animals. The animals were becoming thinner every day. They have tried looking around for food but it wasn't easy for them to find any as food was scarce.

Tortoise and his family were also passing through the same situation; they were starving. All the animals thought that mother-nature was very angry with them as they had never experienced such situation before, the weather was horrible.

Tortoise, after searching for food around him and not finding any, he decided to go to one of his farm that was very far away from the village, hoping that somehow he might find some food. Taking a bag, he set off.

After a long journey, he came to his farm; there he saw a very tall palm tree he was sure he had never seen there before and there was a river flowing by the side. He looked up at the tree and saw plenty ripped palm nuts. Not minding the risk of him falling down, he began to climb it.

It took him some time to reach the top. When he got there, he began to pluck the fruit and put them in his bag. As he was plucking, one of the nuts fell into the river. Tortoise was annoyed that one of his palm nuts had fallen into the river. He said to himself that he cannot let it go; he must get that nut from the river.

So, he climbed down from the tree, kept his bag by the side of the tree and entered the river to retrieve his nut. But as he swum, the nut kept going deep into the river. Tortoise followed the nut determined to get it. The nut continued to go deep into the river until it entered a house. Tortoise followed the nut into the house.

Inside the house, he saw some strange creatures. He scanned the room for his nut when unexpectedly he saw one of them that who was dressed like a king eating his nut! Tortoise said: "Sir, that nut belongs to me, why are u eating it? You have to pay me for it." The creature's eyes were closed as if to savor the taste of what it was eating. Then he finally opened his eyes and said, "This is the most delicious thing I have ever tasted."

"Sir in my village, there is no food and we are starving. This nut is the food I want me and my family to eat this night." Tortoise seemed sad as he said this. The creature looked at him and felt pity for him. He took out a plate and gave it to tortoise. The plate was a magic plate. He told tortoise that when he gets home, he should gather all his family members in his sitting room, lock every door, put the plate in the middle of the room and call whatever food they want and the plate will produce it for them.

Tortoise looked at the creature carefully, not knowing if he should trust it or not but he still decided to give it a try maybe this will really give him and his family food.

Tortoise took the plate and went home. At home, he gathered all his family members into his sitting room, locked all the doors and put the plate in the middle of the room. Then he said to the plate "Jellof rice", immediately Jellof rice filled the plate. He and his children could not believe their eyes, but anyways, they ate it. One of his children said "pepper chicken", pepper chicken filled the plate. And so it went on and on until they were all satisfied.

After keeping the plate for three days and feeding from it; Tortoise been a kind and generous man took the plate to the King. He explained to the King about the magic plate and how it works. The King was pleased and said he will first try it with his family to know its authenticity. So, he called his family members together in the palace, locked the doors, put the plate in the middle of the room, and started calling different types of food. The plate gave them whatever food they asked for.

After this, all the animals were called to the palace. And did the same thing tortoise told them to do. The plate gave them whatever food they asked for. All the animals ate till they were satisfied. They were so happy and they began to praise tortoise.

Tortoise asked the King if he (the King) could keep the plate, but the King told him that it will be better for him (Tortoise) to keep it, however, he had to bring it to the palace every morning for everyone to eat from it, and so, Tortoise became the keeper of the plate. He kept the plate on the top of the roof of his kitchen that was outside his house where his wife usually cooks, but as they've been feeding from the plate, she hadn't been cooking. So tortoise felt it was safe to keep it there.

One day, Tortoise's wife asked one of the children to go bring something she kept on the top of the roof of the kitchen to dry oblivious that her husband had kept the plate there. The child she sent went there and in the process of trying to reach for what his mother sent him, he mistaken pushed the plate. The plate fell on the ground and split into two. Tortoise heard the noise and rushed out to see what had happened, when he saw that his precious plate was on the ground and broken, he became so angry. He tried to glue the plate together and immediately asked all his family members into his sitting room, he locked the door, placed the plate in the middle of the room and said "Mango", unripe mangoes appeared on the plate. He said "rice", spoiled rice appeared. That was how the plate was giving them what they couldn't eat.

Tortoise was not happy at all. He immediately went to the king with the plate and told him what had happened. To demonstrate what he meant when he said the plate was giving them food that they cannot eat, he locked all the palace doors with the king and other people inside, and began to call food, the plate gave them unripe and spoiled food.

The King told him to take the plate back to

the creature and see if there's something it can do about it. Tortoise went back to the palm tree in his farm, climbed it and began to pluck the palm nut. This time around he did not go with a bag. As he was plucking, and was deliberately throwing it on the ground, to his annoyance, none fell into the river. Finally, one managed to fall at the bank of the river. He climbed down and began to push the nut into the river himself. He pushed and pushed the nut till it went deep and entered the house of the creature. In the house, he saw the creature he saw the first time that looked like a king.

Tortoise stretched his hand with the nut in it towards the creature said, "Sir please take this nut and eat."

The creature not even glancing at him

replied, "I don't want the nut."

Tortoise said almost pleading, "Please sir. You have to eat it."

The creature finally lifted its eyes and looked at Tortoise closely. It slowly collected the nut and said, "Ok, now tell me what brings you here."

Tortoise showed it the broken plate and narrated what had happened.

The creature said. "Ok, I will give you something more powerful than the plate." Tortoise immediately became excited.

The creature brought out a long fine cane from under where it was sitting and gave it to him. He instructed him to gather his family inside his sitting room, lock the doors and windows and call any food they want, the cane will provide it.

Tortoise happily collected the cane, went home and did as the creature instructed. They began to call delicious food for the cane, but instead of food, the cane began to flog all of them. It flogged and flogged them. They were crying and begging the cane to show them mercy. They were in so much pain. After a while, the cane stopped flogging. That night Tortoise who was still in pains thought to himself that the cane can't only flog him and his family. That he must take it to the King.

Early morning the next day, Tortoise took the cane to the King. He told the King that the cane gives more delicious food than the plate and all the King needs to do is to gather every animal together into the palace so they can enjoy the food together. He told the king exactly what the creature told him to do. The king thought it was a good idea. So he summoned every animal to the palace.

Meanwhile, Tortoise took all his family members and climbed a tall tree not too far from the palace. They stayed there and watched what was happening in the palace. The palace doors were tightly locked. And one by one the animals began to call different food for the cane. The cane got up and began to flog them. It flogged and flogged everyone in the room including the King. As everyone was crying and shouting in agony, Tortoise and his family were on the tree laughing very hard.

The cane flogged them for a very long time and suddenly stopped. The animals quickly opened the door and rushed out shouting and cursing Tortoise. The King ordered for Tortoise and his family to be brought to the palace. They searched for him and finally found him and his family hiding on a tree. They brought them to the palace. Tortoise, for allowing the King to be flogged, was punished and banished from the kingdom.

CHAPTER TWO

MR. OKORO AND THE RATS

Mr. Okoro was a well known man who lived in a small village. He was a trader although not rich; he was contented with his life. He lived in a house gifted to him by his father. He was kind to everyone this made most people to like him. The only problem he had was the rats in his house. Those rats had been terrorizing him for a very long time that he had even forgotten how they came to live with him in his house. The rats were not scared of him at all as they sometimes move his things around. There were times that if they see him and he tries to *shoo* them away, they won't run, instead they will stay where they are and just stare at him.

Few times he had tried poisoning them, but

each time he does that, they will eat the poisoned food, steal his pot of food, eat the food in it and make so much noise in the night that will keep him awake throughout the night. They do this to him for one week anytime they sensed that he had used poison on them.

One day, Mr. Okoro was at John's house. John was his friend. They were having a good time and discussing. The topic shifted to Mr. Okoro's predicament.

John: Okoro what are you going to do about those rats in your house?

John looked at his friend feeling pity for him. He had seen what those rats are capable of as he had spent one night there. After that night's horrible experience, he had vowed never to spend any other night there again.

He would rather sleep on the street instead of Mr. Okoro's house.

Mr. Okoro: I can't run away from my house. But ehn, am thinking that those rats are not ordinary rats. They are demons.

John: Of course they are not ordinary. I can still remember the number of times you have used poison on them. The way they behave after eating the poison is really terrifying. If am the one living in that house, I would have ran away from it a long time.

Mr. Okoro: Hahaha! But I am not you. They must leave my house for me and not the other way round.

John: Please don't mock me. Just be

careful. Am sure a solution will com.

Mr. Okoro went home when it was almost getting very late into the night. At home, he took his bath, ate, and before he slept, he prayed to God to protect him from these demons in the form of rats.

Early the next morning, noises woke him up. He got up and looked around to see where the noise was coming from. Lo and behold, he saw some rats carrying his big television on their head. The sight horrified him. He ran out of his house in terror shouting, "Somebody help me oooh, those rats want to carry everything in my house and chase me away. They want to kill me oooh!" He kept shouting and asking anyone he meets on the road for help. People were just staring at him. Although most of them knew about the rats in his house, they still stood watching him and wondering what the rats have done to him again.

In his hysteric search for help, he saw a man from afar dressed in white. Mr. Okoro ran up to him. The man looked mysterious and wore a mischievous smile. He was carrying different funny looking whistles on him. The whistles were in different shapes and colours. Mr Okoro began to plead, "Please help me. The rats in my house are demons. They are on a mission to steal everything in my house and drive me away. They are driving me crazy. Please help me!"

The man started laughing hysterically. He suddenly stopped, putting on a serious look, he said, "I am the one that takes care of rats. They fear me because I have some magical things they hate." Then he took out one of the whistles, a red one and said, "Take this whistle, all you have to do is to blow it immediately you get home, but first make sure you open all your doors and windows leading to outside your house. When they hear the noise from this whistle, they will all run away from your house and never come back again."

Mr. Okoro quickly collected the whistle and thanked him before running back home. When he got home, he peeped inside the house to see what the rats were doing. But he only saw his television in one corner of the room where the rats had left it and the rats were nowhere in sight. He slowly walked in, and then began to open his doors and windows that led to outside his house.

He sat down and blew the whistle.

Suddenly all the rats began to franticly tear his cloths in one of his bag he had left opened. Each rat tore a piece from any cloth they touched, tied the piece around their waist. In no time, they were all on a straight line and began to dance, moving towards Mr. Okoro. Seeing this, Mr. Okoro was really scared out of his wits. He ran out of his house shouting, "Those rats have gone crazy, somebody please save me ooo!"

Many people were outside and were watching him. They began to whisper to themselves. They were saying that maybe it was Mr. Okoro that had really gone crazy. No one tried to neither talk to him nor help him as they all avoided him.

Mr. Okoro, after running for a while and

shouting, he finally saw the mysterious man he had seen before. The mysterious man was coming to him. When he got to Mr. Okoro, he began to laugh uncontrollably. He stopped and began talking seriously, "My customer, have you ever gone to buy something and didn't even bother to ask how much the cost is or even paying for the item before running off to use it? Well, I gave you the wrong whistle because I knew you would not pay me." He began to laugh again, and said in between his laughter, "those rats must have scared you……hahahaha…."

Mr. Okoro, who was calm now, just stared at him speechlessly. He asked how much for the whistles. He paid for them and the mysterious man gave him a white whistle, he told Mr. Okoro to keep the red whistle as he will need it in the future. He gave him the same instruction as the first one on how to use the white whistle. Mr. Okoro went home and blew the whistle. All the rats scrambled out of the house quickly as each one tried to outrun the other. Some ran out through the window while others through the door. It was like there was a huge fire in the house that was chasing them.

After the rat incident, Mr. Okoro got married and had children. He and his family lived happily ever after.

CHAPTER THREE

WHY IS FOWL USED FOR SACRIFICE?

Once upon a time, in the land of the animals, every animal lived happily and in harmony. Their land was fertile and fruitful thus, there was abundance of food. Suddenly, everything began to change. Humans were now coming to hunt them. Many of them couldn't go to the farm anymore as they were scared for their lives. Since many of the animals were no longer going to the farm anymore and planting, food began to get scarce.

However, only Fowl, Duck and their families were not scared of going to their farms as they believed they were too smart to be caught by the humans. Every other animal had warned them to be very careful so as not to be trapped and captured by the humans. As luck would have it, they kept going to their respective farms and planting and harvesting for a long time but they were never caught. When they harvest their crops, they sell it to the other animals at a fair price.

One day, Duck's luck ran out as three of his children were captured by the humans. He and the rest of his family members barely escaped. Since that day, Duck and his family stopped going to the farm. When Fowl heard of this, he laughed and said that Duck was not smart enough and that was why his children were capture. He boosted that he can never be caught by the humans.

As time flew by, things were really becoming tough for them as Fowl was the only one going to the farm; he sold his produce at a high price to them. The elders couldn't take this anymore; they decided to call for a meeting among themselves. During the meeting, it was concluded that they would go to Old Koko the Tortoise who was a powerful spiritual doctor for divination. Maybe there will be a solution to their present predicament.

Old Koko lives at the far end of the kingdom. It took them four hours to get there. At Old Koko's, after the incantation, he told them that the solution to their problem is in their hands; and that among the animals, one of them must volunteer for him and his family to be used for sacrifice annually to appease the gods and the humans. This means that every year, one member of the volunteer's family will be used for sacrifice. The elders went home, each in deep thought as they keep wondering who will really give himself away as sacrifice for all of them. On getting home, they sent out the town crier to announce a meeting at the village square the next morning and every animal must be there.

The next morning, every animal was preparing to go to the village square but Fowl who was too busy with his farm and can never spare his time for such meeting was preparing to go to his farm with his family. The people began to walk to the village square, some in group while some alone. They were discussing possible reasons for the meeting and hoped dearly that a solution for their situation had come.

However, while every animal was on their way to the village square, Fowl and his family were hurrying to their farm. Rabbit and Duck happened to see Fowl and his family with farming tools and in the direction of their farm. They called out to him and ran up to him. When they approached him, Rabbit said:

"My friend I can see that you are heading to your farm. Why are you not going to the village square? You know that this meeting is very important. You can still go to the farm after the meeting."

Fowl replied: Yes Rabbit I know, but you see, we don't know when the meeting will be over. The weeds on my farm are affecting my crops. I and my family want to go remove them.

Duck starred at Fowl really hard and said, "So this farm is more important than the meeting. You don't know what will be discussed there. You don't know if it's a solution to this our problem. Is it because the problem is not affecting you?"

Rabbit wanted to say something, but Fowl cut him off and hurriedly said, "Please my friends whatever decision that is made at the village square, I and my family agree and accept it." Fowl didn't wait for Rabbit and Duck to say anything again as he just hurried off to catch up with his family.

Duck and Rabbit stared at Fowl in bewilderment as his figure disappeared in the distance of his farm.

At the village square, the elders told the animals about their visit to Old Koko's shrine and the outcome of it:

Elder 1: "Old Koko who we all know to be a powerful spiritual doctor said we have to sacrifice to appease the gods and human but the sacrifice is not an ordinary one. One of us has to be used for the sacrifice."

He stopped talking as he wanted what he had said to sink into the mind of the animals. After some moments, another elder began to speak:

Elder 2: "And this sacrifice is to be made annually. Anyone that volunteers, each year one person from his family will be sacrificed. The entire kingdom will take care of every of his needs and help train his children. He will also be considered a hero."

He paused and then asked the vital question:

> "Who will volunteer for him and his family to be used as a sacrifice to stop this calamity from consuming all of us?"

This time around, a terrifying silence swept over the place as everyone was afraid to make any noise not even to move their body. After a long time of silence, another elder spoke:

Elder 3: "Is this how we all will perish? Is there no one willing to save us from this doom?"

Everyone began to look at one another in silence, each hoping that the other will volunteer. After a while, the third elder was about to speak when Rabbit shot his hands up and said "Please hear me." Everyone turned to look at him. "This morning as we were all coming to this place, I and Duck met Fowl on his way to his farm. He told us that he and his family accept whatever decision that is made here, therefore he has accepted to be used for the sacrifice." He looked at Duck and Duck immediately chimed in: "Yes it is true."

There was a moment of silence as everyone sighed in relieve. Then they began to cheer and praise Fowl. They immediately went to Fowl's farm with a rope. They tied the rope on his neck and began to drag him on the ground round the village. Fowl's family were crying and following them. All this while Fowl was protesting and saying that he and his family did not accept to be used for sacrifice but the elders and everyone kept telling him that the decision have already been made and there was no going back.

As Fowl was being dragged, Parrot sat on a tree watching them. He began to laugh loudly and said, "How ridiculous Fowl looks with a rope tied around his neck. It doesn't fit him at all." On hearing this, the animals started whispering among themselves and they thought Fowl really looked ridiculous. They untied the rope around his neck and tied it to his leg, and took him to where he is to be sacrificed.

This is why till this day, Fowl is used for sacrifice and rope is never tied to its neck but on its leg.

www.ingramcontent.com/pod-product-compliance
Lightning Source LLC
Chambersburg PA
CBHW050321220526
45465CB00005B/2081